ROLL-A-PROMPT WRITING JOURNAL

GENRE MASHUP EDITION

MELISSA BANCZAK

LISA MAHONEY

Melissa -
Smoochous to Mark

Lisa -
For David who makes me laugh every day (and who would kill me if I sent him smoochous)

ABOUT THE AUTHORS

In another lifetime, Melissa Banczak was an editor, ghost writer and literary agent specializing in screenplays. She writes the June Nash Mystery series and has a podcast called Books Cubed where she interviews the indie authors you should be reading. Her favorite games involve dice.

In this lifetime, Lisa Mahoney is an award-winning short story writer, adjunct English professor, and most importantly a dreamer. She hides her secret happiness when the power goes out and the generator won't work and her family is forced to play board games with her. She has just completed her first novel.

WHY WE WROTE THIS BOOK

Writers have imaginations. We play the *what-if* and *I-wonder-whether* games that make many of the realists around us scrunch up their noses. But sometimes we get stuck and our imaginations need to find a side door or a backdoor or even a trapdoor—a new way in to our stories. Once in, there's no telling where our creativity will take us. But how do we find those hidden passageways and allay our *stuckness*?

Many depend on prompt books. We're no different yet we yearned to have a *different approach*. So in our efforts to jumpstart our own writing and fire up our fantasies, we turned to our love of games and the randomness of dice and the Roll-A-Prompt Journal Series was born.

Use it alone or with friends. With over 6000 possible combinations, it's the perfect way to get your creative juices flowing.

Melissa & Lisa

HOW TO USE THIS BOOK

Each Roll-A-Prompt Writing Journal features 30 sets of elements that, with the roll of a dice, will create over 6000 prompts per book. What you'll need:

- Pen or pencil
- Dice (or trace the pattern on the next page)
- Imagination

Every story has a Main Character (referred to here as the MC) who drives the action. Each prompt begins with your character roll. After that, you'll get 2 of these 5 elements:

Trait | Location | Object | Word | Scenario

Roll for each selection and then jot it all down at the top of a work page. Once you have your prompt, let your imagination run wild.

A *late woman* doesn't just have to be someone running behind. She could also be pregnant. Or dead.

A *pizza delivery driver* is not just a job designation. It's also a treasure trove of stuff. They'd probably have a car. A phone. Some pizza. Use what you want. It's your prompt.

The paperback has 5 journal sheets per set so you can start writing. The ebook version includes a downloadable PDF.

Want to get even more out of this book? Turn to a random page for your first element. Another for your second. A third for the last. Voila! A new prompt.

So roll your dice, get writing, and above all, have fun!

Melissa & Lisa

We'd love to know how the prompts worked out for you. Did you start a story? Finish one? Publish? Did you try this with your writing group? Email us at mel@melissabanczak.com

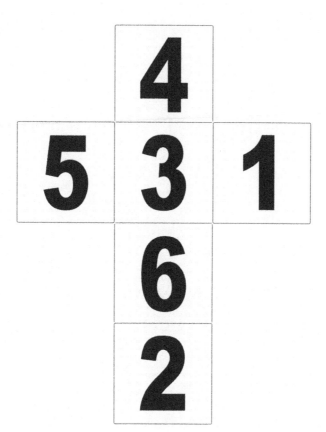

STORY DEVELOPMENT

Character
Roll 1 Number

1. Pixie with a grudge
2. Little league coach
3. Mortuary make-up artist
4. Alligator wrestler
5. Woman from 1620
6. Elderly werewolf

Trait
Roll 1 Number

1. Honest
2. Boorish
3. Charming smile
4. Tidy
5. Idyllic
6. Stingy

Location
Roll 1 Number

1. Farmer's market
2. Long range space telescope
3. Sidewalk cafe
4. Abandoned house
5. Dusty road
6. Pick-your-own-peach orchard

Character_____Trait_____
Location_____

_____
_____
_____
_____
_____
_____
_____
_____
_____
_____
_____
_____
_____
_____
_____
_____
_____
_____
_____
_____
_____
_____
_____
_____
_____
_____
_____
_____
_____
_____

Character_____Trait_____
Location_____

Character_____Trait_____
Location_____

_____
_____
_____
_____
_____
_____
_____
_____
_____
_____
_____
_____
_____
_____
_____
_____
_____
_____
_____
_____
_____
_____
_____
_____
_____
_____
_____
_____
_____
_____
_____
_____
_____
_____
_____
_____
_____

Character_____Trait_____
Location_____

_____
_____
_____
_____
_____
_____
_____
_____
_____
_____
_____
_____
_____
_____
_____
_____
_____
_____
_____
_____
_____
_____
_____
_____
_____
_____
_____
_____
_____
_____
_____
_____
_____

Character_____Trait_____
Location_____

_____
_____
_____
_____
_____
_____
_____
_____
_____
_____
_____
_____
_____
_____
_____
_____
_____
_____
_____
_____
_____
_____
_____
_____
_____
_____
_____
_____
_____
_____
_____
_____

STORY DEVELOPMENT

Character
Roll 1 Number

1. Spy
2. Ob-gyn
3. Meter reader
4. Priest
5. Boxer
6. White stag

Object
Roll 1 Number

1. Tumbleweed
2. Magic 8 ball
3. Amulet
4. Bathroom scale
5. Harness
6. Cell phone charger

Scenario
Roll 1 Number

1. Séance
2. An unattended motel front desk
3. Deep in a hedge maze
4. Computer begins to hack human minds
5. On a stakeout
6. A clay statue goes missing from an archeological dig

Character _____ Object _____
Scenario _____

_____
_____
_____
_____
_____
_____
_____
_____
_____
_____
_____
_____
_____
_____
_____
_____
_____
_____
_____
_____
_____
_____
_____
_____
_____
_____
_____
_____
_____
_____
_____
_____
_____

Character _____Object_____
Scenario _____

Character _____ Object_____

Scenario _____

_____

_____

_____

_____

_____

_____

_____

_____

_____

_____

_____

_____

_____

_____

_____

_____

_____

_____

_____

_____

_____

_____

_____

_____

_____

_____

_____

_____

_____

_____

_____

_____

Character _____Object_____
Scenario _____

_____
_____
_____
_____
_____
_____
_____
_____
_____
_____
_____
_____
_____
_____
_____
_____
_____
_____
_____
_____
_____
_____
_____
_____
_____
_____
_____
_____
_____
_____

Character _____ Object _____

Scenario _____

_____
_____
_____
_____
_____
_____
_____
_____
_____
_____
_____
_____
_____
_____
_____
_____
_____
_____
_____
_____
_____
_____
_____
_____
_____
_____
_____
_____
_____
_____
_____
_____

Character
Roll 1 Number

1. Robotics engineer
2. Starving peasant
3. Crypt robber
4. Ballroom dancer
5. Knife thrower
6. Insomniac

Object
Roll 1 Number

1. 10 lb bag of potatoes
2. Flat tire
3. Gold nugget
4. Night vision goggles
5. Hair dryer
6. Antiseptic

Word
Roll 1 Number

1. Alibi
2. Enormous
3. Masterpiece
4. Pointless
5. Intrigue
6. Dematerialize

Character_____

Object _____Word _____

_____
_____
_____
_____
_____
_____
_____
_____
_____
_____
_____
_____
_____
_____
_____
_____
_____
_____
_____
_____
_____
_____
_____
_____
_____
_____
_____
_____
_____
_____
_____
_____

Character_____

Object _____Word _____

Character_____

Object _____Word _____

_____
_____
_____
_____
_____
_____
_____
_____
_____
_____
_____
_____
_____
_____
_____
_____
_____
_____
_____
_____
_____
_____
_____
_____
_____
_____
_____
_____
_____
_____
_____
_____

Character_____

Object _____Word _____

_____
_____
_____
_____
_____
_____
_____
_____
_____
_____
_____
_____
_____
_____
_____
_____
_____
_____
_____
_____
_____
_____
_____
_____
_____
_____
_____
_____
_____
_____
_____

Character_____

Object _____Word _____

_____
_____
_____
_____
_____
_____
_____
_____
_____
_____
_____
_____
_____
_____
_____
_____
_____
_____
_____
_____
_____
_____
_____
_____
_____
_____
_____
_____
_____
_____
_____
_____
_____
_____

STORY DEVELOPMENT

Character
Roll 1 Number

1. Leprechaun
2. Shadow figure
3. Mall gift wrapper
4. Coin collector
5. Pickpocket
6. Fallen angel

Word
Roll 1 Number

1. Aroma
2. Opinion
3. Priory
4. Medicinal
5. Vulnerable
6. Enchanted

Scenario
Roll 1 Number

1. Searching for a lost cat
2. Bird diving into a lake comes up with a skull
3. On a ghost tour
4. Preacher gathers his congregation for bad news
5. Shuttle is about to launch
6. Data starts disappearing from a computer screen

Character_____Word_____
Scenario_____

_____
_____
_____
_____
_____
_____
_____
_____
_____
_____
_____
_____
_____
_____
_____
_____
_____
_____
_____
_____
_____
_____
_____
_____
_____
_____
_____
_____
_____
_____
_____
_____
_____
_____
_____
_____
_____

Character_____Word_____
Scenario_____

_____
_____
_____
_____
_____
_____
_____
_____
_____
_____
_____
_____
_____
_____
_____
_____
_____
_____
_____
_____
_____
_____
_____
_____
_____
_____
_____
_____
_____
_____
_____
_____
_____
_____
_____
_____
_____
_____
_____

Character_____Word_____
Scenario_____

_____
_____
_____
_____
_____
_____
_____
_____
_____
_____
_____
_____
_____
_____
_____
_____
_____
_____
_____
_____
_____
_____
_____
_____
_____
_____
_____
_____
_____
_____
_____
_____
_____
_____
_____
_____
_____

Character_____Word_____
Scenario_____

_____
_____
_____
_____
_____
_____
_____
_____
_____
_____
_____
_____
_____
_____
_____
_____
_____
_____
_____
_____
_____
_____
_____
_____
_____
_____
_____
_____
_____
_____

Character_____Word_____
Scenario_____

_____
_____
_____
_____
_____
_____
_____
_____
_____
_____
_____
_____
_____
_____
_____
_____
_____
_____
_____
_____
_____
_____
_____
_____
_____
_____
_____
_____
_____
_____
_____
_____
_____
_____
_____

Character
Roll 1 Number

1. Barista
2. Pizza delivery driver
3. Glassblower
4. 500-year-old witch
5. Astronaut with first signs of dementia
6. Live mannequin

Mood
Roll 1 Number

1. Spontaneous
2. Reflective
3. Electricity in the air
4. Anguished
5. Guilty
6. Jealous

Word
Roll 1 Number

1. Tell-all
2. Zesty
3. Hyperdrive
4. Deception
5. Nothing
6. Missing

Character_____

Mood_____Word _____

Character_____

Mood_____Word _____

_____
_____
_____
_____
_____
_____
_____
_____
_____
_____
_____
_____
_____
_____
_____
_____
_____
_____
_____
_____
_____
_____
_____
_____
_____
_____
_____
_____
_____
_____
_____
_____
_____

Character_____

Mood_____Word _____

Character_____

Mood_____Word _____

_____
_____
_____
_____
_____
_____
_____
_____
_____
_____
_____
_____
_____
_____
_____
_____
_____
_____
_____
_____
_____
_____
_____
_____
_____
_____
_____
_____
_____
_____
_____

Character_____

Mood_____Word _____

_____
_____
_____
_____
_____
_____
_____
_____
_____
_____
_____
_____
_____
_____
_____
_____
_____
_____
_____
_____
_____
_____
_____
_____
_____
_____
_____
_____
_____
_____
_____
_____
_____
_____
_____

Character
Roll 1 number
Even = MC is alone
Odd = Roll again for a companion

1. Birthday party clown
2. Tree trimmer
3. Ambassador
4. Fishmonger
5. Gatekeeper in purgatory
6. Romance novel writer

IF the MC is alone, add an object
Roll 1 Number

1. Hard boiled egg
2. Cowbell
3. Mirror
4. Stuffed hedgehog
5. Oxygen tank
6. Nose-ring

Scenario
Roll 1 number

1. Called for jury duty
2. Abandoned cart at the supermarket
3. Screams echo through the ship
4. Lost in a passageway
5. Unmanned horse and buggy
6. Dog is found in a tree house

Character(s)_____

Object_____

Scenario_____

_____
_____
_____
_____
_____
_____
_____
_____
_____
_____
_____
_____
_____
_____
_____
_____
_____
_____
_____
_____
_____
_____
_____
_____
_____
_____
_____
_____
_____
_____
_____
_____
_____

Character(s)_____

Object_____

Scenario_____

_____
_____
_____
_____
_____
_____
_____
_____
_____
_____
_____
_____
_____
_____
_____
_____
_____
_____
_____
_____
_____
_____
_____
_____
_____
_____
_____
_____
_____
_____
_____
_____
_____
_____
_____

Character(s)_____

Object_____

Scenario_____

_____

_____

_____

_____

_____

_____

_____

_____

_____

_____

_____

_____

_____

_____

_____

_____

_____

_____

_____

_____

_____

_____

_____

_____

_____

_____

_____

_____

_____

Character(s)_____

Object_____

Scenario_____

_____
_____
_____
_____
_____
_____
_____
_____
_____
_____
_____
_____
_____
_____
_____
_____
_____
_____
_____
_____
_____
_____
_____
_____
_____
_____
_____
_____
_____
_____
_____
_____

Character(s)_____

Object_____

Scenario_____

_____
_____
_____
_____
_____
_____
_____
_____
_____
_____
_____
_____
_____
_____
_____
_____
_____
_____
_____
_____
_____
_____
_____
_____
_____
_____
_____
_____
_____
_____
_____
_____
_____

STORY DEVELOPMENT

Character
Roll 1 Number

1. College student
2. Hairdresser
3. Botanist
4. Mapmaker
5. Foreign exchange student
6. Pregnant ghost

Trait
Roll 1 Number

1. Crisp
2. Poetic
3. Fawning
4. Disobedient
5. Strange
6. Neurotic

Location
Roll 1 Number

1. Nest of eggs deep in a cave
2. Bonfire
3. Under a weeping willow tree
4. Crowded elevator
5. Rooftop pigeon roost
6. Diner counter

Character_____Trait_____
Location_____

_____
_____
_____
_____
_____
_____
_____
_____
_____
_____
_____
_____
_____
_____
_____
_____
_____
_____
_____
_____
_____
_____
_____
_____
_____
_____
_____
_____
_____
_____
_____

Character_____Trait_____
Location_____

_____
_____
_____
_____
_____
_____
_____
_____
_____
_____
_____
_____
_____
_____
_____
_____
_____
_____
_____
_____
_____
_____
_____
_____
_____
_____
_____
_____
_____
_____
_____
_____
_____
_____

Character_____Trait_____
Location_____

_____
_____
_____
_____
_____
_____
_____
_____
_____
_____
_____
_____
_____
_____
_____
_____
_____
_____
_____
_____
_____
_____
_____
_____
_____
_____
_____
_____
_____
_____
_____
_____
_____

Character_____Trait_____
Location_____

_____
_____
_____
_____
_____
_____
_____
_____
_____
_____
_____
_____
_____
_____
_____
_____
_____
_____
_____
_____
_____
_____
_____
_____
_____
_____
_____
_____
_____
_____
_____
_____
_____
_____
_____

Character_____Trait_____
Location_____

_____
_____
_____
_____
_____
_____
_____
_____
_____
_____
_____
_____
_____
_____
_____
_____
_____
_____
_____
_____
_____
_____
_____
_____
_____
_____
_____
_____
_____
_____
_____
_____
_____
_____

STORY DEVELOPMENT

Character
Roll 1 Number

1. Soldier on a secret mission
2. Faceless man
3. Blind child
4. Cake decorator
5. Meteorologist
6. Lycanthrope

Object
Roll 1 Number

1. Simulated sunshine
2. Battery
3. Poem
4. Deck of tarot cards
5. Extension cord
6. Tusk

Scenario
Roll 1 Number

1. Cave's opening collapses
2. Waking up with sleep paralysis
3. Bay doors malfunction during a spacewalk
4. Police lineup
5. Given the wrong coffee order
6. Tide rolls in

Character _____Object_____

Scenario _____

_____

_____

_____

_____

_____

_____

_____

_____

_____

_____

_____

_____

_____

_____

_____

_____

_____

_____

_____

_____

_____

_____

_____

_____

_____

_____

_____

_____

_____

_____

_____

Character _____ Object _____
Scenario _____

_____
_____
_____
_____
_____
_____
_____
_____
_____
_____
_____
_____
_____
_____
_____
_____
_____
_____
_____
_____
_____
_____
_____
_____
_____
_____
_____
_____
_____
_____
_____
_____
_____
_____

Character _____Object_____

Scenario _____

_____
_____
_____
_____
_____
_____
_____
_____
_____
_____
_____
_____
_____
_____
_____
_____
_____
_____
_____
_____
_____
_____
_____
_____
_____
_____
_____
_____
_____
_____
_____
_____
_____

Character _____Object_____

Scenario _____

_____
_____
_____
_____
_____
_____
_____
_____
_____
_____
_____
_____
_____
_____
_____
_____
_____
_____
_____
_____
_____
_____
_____
_____
_____
_____
_____
_____
_____
_____
_____
_____

Character _____Object_____

Scenario _____

_____

_____

_____

_____

_____

_____

_____

_____

_____

_____

_____

_____

_____

_____

_____

_____

_____

_____

_____

_____

_____

_____

_____

_____

_____

_____

_____

_____

_____

_____

_____

Character
Roll 1 Number

1. Artist
2. 12 year-old possessed boy
3. Stalker
4. Empath
5. Flight attendant
6. Girl with a meatball

Object
Roll 1 Number

1. Tape recorder
2. Christmas tree
3. Knee brace
4. Protein bar
5. Girdle
6. Snow globe

Word
Roll 1 Number

1. Toil
2. Antiquity
3. Echo
4. Reserve
5. Grace
6. Locate

Character_____

Object _____Word _____

_____
_____
_____
_____
_____
_____
_____
_____
_____
_____
_____
_____
_____
_____
_____
_____
_____
_____
_____
_____
_____
_____
_____
_____
_____
_____
_____
_____
_____
_____
_____
_____
_____
_____

Character_____

Object _____Word _____

Character_____

Object _____Word _____

_____
_____
_____
_____
_____
_____
_____
_____
_____
_____
_____
_____
_____
_____
_____
_____
_____
_____
_____
_____
_____
_____
_____
_____
_____
_____
_____
_____
_____
_____
_____

Character_____

Object _____Word _____

_____
_____
_____
_____
_____
_____
_____
_____
_____
_____
_____
_____
_____
_____
_____
_____
_____
_____
_____
_____
_____
_____
_____
_____
_____
_____
_____
_____
_____
_____
_____
_____

Character_____

Object _____Word _____

_____
_____
_____
_____
_____
_____
_____
_____
_____
_____
_____
_____
_____
_____
_____
_____
_____
_____
_____
_____
_____
_____
_____
_____
_____
_____
_____
_____
_____
_____
_____
_____

STORY DEVELOPMENT

Character
Roll 1 Number

1. Acupuncturist
2. World traveler
3. Graffiti artist
4. Linguist
5. Sand king
6. Female swordmaster

Word
Roll 1 Number

1. Starchart
2. Rash
3. Moist
4. Hibernation
5. Awaken
6. Empire

Scenario
Roll 1 Number

1. Overnight at a sleep apnea clinic
2. Stone steps rise from the water
3. Patient in body bag sits up
4. Landing party materializes on the edge of a sheer cliff
5. Auditioning for a talent show
6. Train hits a car parked on the tracks

Character_____Word_____
Scenario_____

_____
_____
_____
_____
_____
_____
_____
_____
_____
_____
_____
_____
_____
_____
_____
_____
_____
_____
_____
_____
_____
_____
_____
_____
_____
_____
_____
_____
_____
_____
_____
_____
_____

Character_____Word_____
Scenario_____

_____
_____
_____
_____
_____
_____
_____
_____
_____
_____
_____
_____
_____
_____
_____
_____
_____
_____
_____
_____
_____
_____
_____
_____
_____
_____
_____
_____
_____
_____
_____
_____
_____
_____

Character_____Word_____

Scenario_____

_____
_____
_____
_____
_____
_____
_____
_____
_____
_____
_____
_____
_____
_____
_____
_____
_____
_____
_____
_____
_____
_____
_____
_____
_____
_____
_____
_____
_____
_____
_____
_____
_____

Character_____Word_____
Scenario_____

_____
_____
_____
_____
_____
_____
_____
_____
_____
_____
_____
_____
_____
_____
_____
_____
_____
_____
_____
_____
_____
_____
_____
_____
_____
_____
_____
_____
_____
_____
_____
_____
_____
_____
_____
_____

Character_____Word_____

Scenario_____

_____
_____
_____
_____
_____
_____
_____
_____
_____
_____
_____
_____
_____
_____
_____
_____
_____
_____
_____
_____
_____
_____
_____
_____
_____
_____
_____
_____
_____
_____
_____
_____
_____
_____
_____
_____

Character
Roll 1 Number

1. Florist
2. 4-year-old piano prodigy
3. Culinary specialist
4. Gorgon
5. Blacksmith
6. Dog food tester

Mood
Roll 1 Number

1. Disillusioned
2. Weepy
3. Sarcastic
4. Overcast sky
5. Pouty
6. Frail

Word
Roll 1 Number

1. Rehab
2. Juicy
3. Anti-gravitational
4. Vanished
5. Locate
6. Treasure

Character_____

Mood_____Word _____

_____
_____
_____
_____
_____
_____
_____
_____
_____
_____
_____
_____
_____
_____
_____
_____
_____
_____
_____
_____
_____
_____
_____
_____
_____
_____
_____
_____
_____
_____
_____
_____
_____
_____

Character_____

Mood_____Word _____

Character_____

Mood_____Word _____

Character_____

Mood_____Word _____

_____
_____
_____
_____
_____
_____
_____
_____
_____
_____
_____
_____
_____
_____
_____
_____
_____
_____
_____
_____
_____
_____
_____
_____
_____
_____
_____
_____
_____
_____
_____
_____

Character_____

Mood_____Word _____

_____
_____
_____
_____
_____
_____
_____
_____
_____
_____
_____
_____
_____
_____
_____
_____
_____
_____
_____
_____
_____
_____
_____
_____
_____
_____
_____
_____
_____
_____
_____
_____
_____
_____

Character
Roll 1 number
Even = MC is alone
Odd = Roll again for a companion

1. Shapeshifter
2. Heir to candy store
3. Guard on a break
4. Voodoo priest
5. Man with two camels
6. Newbie to space

IF the MC is alone, add an object
Roll 1 Number

1. Gummy vitamins
2. Kite
3. Compass
4. Packing tape
5. Herb
6. Tweezers

Scenario
Roll 1 number

1. Waiting for a washer at the laundromat
2. Finding a felt marker in the gutter
3. Out for a walk during a meteor shower
4. Pie-eating contest
5. Dry cleaning comes back with the key to a safe deposit box in the pocket
6. Funeral home during a wake on Halloween

Character(s)_____

Object_____

Scenario_____

_____
_____
_____
_____
_____
_____
_____
_____
_____
_____
_____
_____
_____
_____
_____
_____
_____
_____
_____
_____
_____
_____
_____
_____
_____
_____
_____
_____
_____
_____
_____
_____

Character(s)_____

Object_____

Scenario_____

_____

_____

_____

_____

_____

_____

_____

_____

_____

_____

_____

_____

_____

_____

_____

_____

_____

_____

_____

_____

_____

_____

_____

_____

_____

_____

_____

_____

_____

_____

_____

_____

Character(s)_____

Object_____

Scenario_____

_____
_____
_____
_____
_____
_____
_____
_____
_____
_____
_____
_____
_____
_____
_____
_____
_____
_____
_____
_____
_____
_____
_____
_____
_____
_____
_____
_____
_____
_____
_____

Character(s)_____

Object_____

Scenario_____

_____
_____
_____
_____
_____
_____
_____
_____
_____
_____
_____
_____
_____
_____
_____
_____
_____
_____
_____
_____
_____
_____
_____
_____
_____
_____
_____
_____
_____
_____
_____
_____
_____
_____

Character(s)_____

Object_____

Scenario_____

_____
_____
_____
_____
_____
_____
_____
_____
_____
_____
_____
_____
_____
_____
_____
_____
_____
_____
_____
_____
_____
_____
_____
_____
_____
_____
_____
_____
_____
_____
_____

STORY DEVELOPMENT

Character
Roll 1 Number

1. Fey
2. 70-something man
3. Woman tending a garden
4. Salsa dancer
5. Hyperactive spirit
6. Henna artist

Trait
Roll 1 Number

1. Grim
2. Helpful
3. Obedient
4. Regal
5. Persnickety
6. Giggly

Location
Roll 1 Number

1. Subterranean tunnel
2. Lake of acid
3. 4th of July fireworks
4. Outhouse
5. Abandoned house
6. Dental office

Character_____Trait_____
Location_____

_____
_____
_____
_____
_____
_____
_____
_____
_____
_____
_____
_____
_____
_____
_____
_____
_____
_____
_____
_____
_____
_____
_____
_____
_____
_____
_____
_____
_____
_____
_____
_____
_____

Character_____Trait_____
Location_____

_____
_____
_____
_____
_____
_____
_____
_____
_____
_____
_____
_____
_____
_____
_____
_____
_____
_____
_____
_____
_____
_____
_____
_____
_____
_____
_____
_____
_____
_____
_____
_____
_____
_____
_____

Character_____Trait_____
Location_____

_____
_____
_____
_____
_____
_____
_____
_____
_____
_____
_____
_____
_____
_____
_____
_____
_____
_____
_____
_____
_____
_____
_____
_____
_____
_____
_____
_____
_____
_____
_____
_____
_____
_____

Character_____Trait_____
Location_____

_____
_____
_____
_____
_____
_____
_____
_____
_____
_____
_____
_____
_____
_____
_____
_____
_____
_____
_____
_____
_____
_____
_____
_____
_____
_____
_____
_____
_____
_____
_____
_____
_____
_____

Character_____Trait_____
Location_____

_____
_____
_____
_____
_____
_____
_____
_____
_____
_____
_____
_____
_____
_____
_____
_____
_____
_____
_____
_____
_____
_____
_____
_____
_____
_____
_____
_____
_____
_____
_____
_____
_____
_____
_____
_____

STORY DEVELOPMENT

Character
Roll 1 Number

1. Bank robber
2. Teenage boy with telekinesis
3. Fire breather
4. Oceanographer
5. Police dispatcher
6. Dance instructor

Object
Roll 1 Number

1. Walkie talkie
2. Large deli pickle
3. Sweatband
4. One credit
5. Broadsword
6. Geiger counter

Scenario
Roll 1 Number

1. Stuck in an airplane bathroom
2. MC answers phone and hears own voice
3. An alpaca escapes from a petting zoo
4. Unsigned letter is delivered
5. Lake has thickened like gelatin
6. Buzzing insects disturb a pleasant Sunday morning

Character _____Object_____

Scenario _____

_____
_____
_____
_____
_____
_____
_____
_____
_____
_____
_____
_____
_____
_____
_____
_____
_____
_____
_____
_____
_____
_____
_____
_____
_____
_____
_____
_____
_____
_____
_____
_____
_____

Character _____ Object_____

Scenario _____

_____

_____

_____

_____

_____

_____

_____

_____

_____

_____

_____

_____

_____

_____

_____

_____

_____

_____

_____

_____

_____

_____

_____

_____

_____

_____

_____

_____

_____

_____

_____

_____

_____

_____

_____

Character _____Object_____

Scenario _____

_____
_____
_____
_____
_____
_____
_____
_____
_____
_____
_____
_____
_____
_____
_____
_____
_____
_____
_____
_____
_____
_____
_____
_____
_____
_____
_____
_____
_____
_____
_____

Character _____Object_____

Scenario _____

_____
_____
_____
_____
_____
_____
_____
_____
_____
_____
_____
_____
_____
_____
_____
_____
_____
_____
_____
_____
_____
_____
_____
_____
_____
_____
_____
_____
_____
_____

Character _____Object_____

Scenario _____

_____
_____
_____
_____
_____
_____
_____
_____
_____
_____
_____
_____
_____
_____
_____
_____
_____
_____
_____
_____
_____
_____
_____
_____
_____
_____
_____
_____
_____
_____
_____
_____
_____
_____

CHARACTER DEVELOPMENT

Character
Roll 1 Number

1. Moon worshipper
2. Hypnotist
3. Engineer with a stomach ache
4. Woman with a carnation
5. Beekeeper
6. Locksmith

Object
Roll 1 Number

1. DNA sample
2. Cursed book
3. Rolling pin
4. Lunchbox
5. Bulletproof vest
6. Quill

Word
Roll 1 Number

1. Infestation
2. Fever
3. Decompression
4. Traditional
5. Holographic
6. Certified

Character_____

Object _____Word _____

_____
_____
_____
_____
_____
_____
_____
_____
_____
_____
_____
_____
_____
_____
_____
_____
_____
_____
_____
_____
_____
_____
_____
_____
_____
_____
_____
_____
_____
_____
_____

Character_____

Object _____Word _____

_____
_____
_____
_____
_____
_____
_____
_____
_____
_____
_____
_____
_____
_____
_____
_____
_____
_____
_____
_____
_____
_____
_____
_____
_____
_____
_____
_____
_____
_____
_____
_____
_____
_____
_____

Character_____

Object _____Word _____

_____
_____
_____
_____
_____
_____
_____
_____
_____
_____
_____
_____
_____
_____
_____
_____
_____
_____
_____
_____
_____
_____
_____
_____
_____
_____
_____
_____
_____
_____
_____
_____

Character_____

Object _____Word _____

Character_____

Object _____Word _____

_____
_____
_____
_____
_____
_____
_____
_____
_____
_____
_____
_____
_____
_____
_____
_____
_____
_____
_____
_____
_____
_____
_____
_____
_____
_____
_____
_____
_____
_____
_____
_____
_____

STORY DEVELOPMENT

Character
Roll 1 Number

1. Mercenary
2. Vet
3. Demon conjuror
4. Brick layer
5. Navigator
6. TV reporter

Word
Roll 1 Number

1. Identity
2. Luscious
3. Retrofit
4. Brimstone
5. Panorama
6. Ancient

Scenario
Roll 1 Number

1. Flock of birds disappears mid-flight
2. Unicorn is trapped
3. Message appears on paper in a typewriter
4. Email confirmation for a reservation never made
5. Walking into a bank robbery
6. Sneaking into a movie theater

Character_____Word_____
Scenario_____

Character_____Word_____
Scenario_____

Character_____Word_____
Scenario_____

_____
_____
_____
_____
_____
_____
_____
_____
_____
_____
_____
_____
_____
_____
_____
_____
_____
_____
_____
_____
_____
_____
_____
_____
_____
_____
_____
_____
_____
_____

Character_____Word_____
Scenario_____

_____
_____
_____
_____
_____
_____
_____
_____
_____
_____
_____
_____
_____
_____
_____
_____
_____
_____
_____
_____
_____
_____
_____
_____
_____
_____
_____
_____
_____
_____

Character_____Word_____
Scenario_____

_____
_____
_____
_____
_____
_____
_____
_____
_____
_____
_____
_____
_____
_____
_____
_____
_____
_____
_____
_____
_____
_____
_____
_____
_____
_____
_____
_____
_____
_____
_____
_____
_____

Character
Roll 1 Number

1. Gambler
2. Rideshare driver
3. Park ranger
4. Ex-con
5. Speech therapist
6. Blogger

Mood
Roll 1 Number

1. Romantic
2. Motivated
3. Apologetic
4. Self-destructive
5. Predatory
6. Livid

Word
Roll 1 Number

1. Narcotic
2. Whodunit
3. Disruptor
4. Fire
5. Justified
6. Enchantment

Character_____
Mood_____Word _____

_____
_____
_____
_____
_____
_____
_____
_____
_____
_____
_____
_____
_____
_____
_____
_____
_____
_____
_____
_____
_____
_____
_____
_____
_____
_____
_____
_____
_____
_____
_____
_____
_____

Character_____

Mood_____Word _____

Character_____

Mood_____Word _____

Character_____

Mood_____Word _____

_____

_____

_____

_____

_____

_____

_____

_____

_____

_____

_____

_____

_____

_____

_____

_____

_____

_____

_____

_____

_____

_____

_____

_____

_____

_____

_____

_____

_____

_____

_____

Character_____

Mood_____Word _____

_____

_____

_____

_____

_____

_____

_____

_____

_____

_____

_____

_____

_____

_____

_____

_____

_____

_____

_____

_____

_____

_____

_____

_____

_____

_____

_____

_____

_____

_____

_____

_____

Character
Roll 1 number
Even = MC is alone
Odd = Roll again for a companion

1. Stand-up comedian
2. Delivery driver
3. First officer
4. Masked horse rider
5. Phoenix
6. Welder

IF the MC is alone, add an object
Roll 1 Number

1. Roll of pennies
2. Embroidered slippers
3. Drone
4. Wedding ring
5. Bag of dirt
6. Syringe

Scenario
Roll 1 number

1. Getting fit for a spacesuit
2. Boss dies in the middle of a job interview
3. Car stalls in the fast food drive-thru
4. Light never turns off
5. Probe is discovered drifting in space
6. Is there a troll under that bridge?

Character(s)_____

Object_____

Scenario_____

_____
_____
_____
_____
_____
_____
_____
_____
_____
_____
_____
_____
_____
_____
_____
_____
_____
_____
_____
_____
_____
_____
_____
_____
_____
_____
_____
_____
_____
_____
_____
_____
_____
_____

Character(s)_____

Object_____

Scenario_____

_____
_____
_____
_____
_____
_____
_____
_____
_____
_____
_____
_____
_____
_____
_____
_____
_____
_____
_____
_____
_____
_____
_____
_____
_____
_____
_____
_____
_____
_____
_____
_____
_____

Character(s)_____

Object_____

Scenario_____

_____
_____
_____
_____
_____
_____
_____
_____
_____
_____
_____
_____
_____
_____
_____
_____
_____
_____
_____
_____
_____
_____
_____
_____
_____
_____
_____
_____
_____
_____
_____
_____
_____

Character(s)_____

Object_____

Scenario_____

_____
_____
_____
_____
_____
_____
_____
_____
_____
_____
_____
_____
_____
_____
_____
_____
_____
_____
_____
_____
_____
_____
_____
_____
_____
_____
_____
_____
_____
_____
_____
_____
_____

Character(s)_____

Object_____

Scenario_____

_____
_____
_____
_____
_____
_____
_____
_____
_____
_____
_____
_____
_____
_____
_____
_____
_____
_____
_____
_____
_____
_____
_____
_____
_____
_____
_____
_____
_____
_____
_____
_____
_____
_____
_____
_____

Character
Roll 1 Number

1. Griffin
2. Amnesia victim
3. Chemistry lab assistant
4. State senator
5. Town historian
6. Lost child

Trait
Roll 1 Number

1. Alert
2. Boisterous
3. Shy
4. Delicate
5. Pissy
6. Chirpy

Location
Roll 1 Number

1. Moat
2. Cryogenic facility
3. Elevator that opens to nothing
4. Root cellar
5. Office copy room
6. Dentist's waiting room

Character_____Trait_____
Location_____

_____
_____
_____
_____
_____
_____
_____
_____
_____
_____
_____
_____
_____
_____
_____
_____
_____
_____
_____
_____
_____
_____
_____
_____
_____
_____
_____
_____
_____
_____
_____
_____

Character_____Trait_____
Location_____

_____
_____
_____
_____
_____
_____
_____
_____
_____
_____
_____
_____
_____
_____
_____
_____
_____
_____
_____
_____
_____
_____
_____
_____
_____
_____
_____
_____
_____
_____
_____
_____

Character_____Trait_____
Location_____

_____
_____
_____
_____
_____
_____
_____
_____
_____
_____
_____
_____
_____
_____
_____
_____
_____
_____
_____
_____
_____
_____
_____
_____
_____
_____
_____
_____
_____
_____
_____

Character_____Trait_____
Location_____

_____
_____
_____
_____
_____
_____
_____
_____
_____
_____
_____
_____
_____
_____
_____
_____
_____
_____
_____
_____
_____
_____
_____
_____
_____
_____
_____
_____
_____
_____
_____

Character_____Trait_____
Location_____

_____
_____
_____
_____
_____
_____
_____
_____
_____
_____
_____
_____
_____
_____
_____
_____
_____
_____
_____
_____
_____
_____
_____
_____
_____
_____
_____
_____
_____
_____
_____
_____
_____
_____

STORY DEVELOPMENT

Character
Roll 1 Number

1. Hotel maid
2. 17-year-old girl
3. Morale officer who hates the job
4. Fairy godmother
5. Paranormal investigator
6. Tattooed man

Object
Roll 1 Number

1. Frisbee
2. Wand
3. Propeller
4. Yoga mat
5. Dart board
6. Earring back

Scenario
Roll 1 Number

1. First contact
2. Campfire in the distance
3. Bloody knife on the counter
4. Arguing with a bully
5. Stood up on a blind date
6. Falling into a ravine

Character _____Object_____

Scenario _____

_____

_____

_____

_____

_____

_____

_____

_____

_____

_____

_____

_____

_____

_____

_____

_____

_____

_____

_____

_____

_____

_____

_____

_____

_____

_____

_____

_____

_____

_____

Character _____ Object _____

Scenario _____

_____
_____
_____
_____
_____
_____
_____
_____
_____
_____
_____
_____
_____
_____
_____
_____
_____
_____
_____
_____
_____
_____
_____
_____
_____
_____
_____
_____
_____
_____
_____
_____
_____
_____
_____

Character _____Object_____

Scenario _____

_____
_____
_____
_____
_____
_____
_____
_____
_____
_____
_____
_____
_____
_____
_____
_____
_____
_____
_____
_____
_____
_____
_____
_____
_____
_____
_____
_____
_____
_____
_____
_____

Character _____Object_____
Scenario _____

_____
_____
_____
_____
_____
_____
_____
_____
_____
_____
_____
_____
_____
_____
_____
_____
_____
_____
_____
_____
_____
_____
_____
_____
_____
_____
_____
_____
_____
_____
_____
_____
_____

Character _____Object_____
Scenario _____

_____
_____
_____
_____
_____
_____
_____
_____
_____
_____
_____
_____
_____
_____
_____
_____
_____
_____
_____
_____
_____
_____
_____
_____
_____
_____
_____
_____
_____
_____
_____
_____
_____
_____
_____
_____

Character
Roll 1 Number

1. Lobster boat captain
2. Essential oils aficionado
3. Tour guide
4. One-eyed owl
5. Prom queen
6. Olympic runner

Object
Roll 1 Number

1. Bullet casing
2. Kitchen timer
3. Gravity boots
4. Mound of ash
5. Lighter
6. Fortune cookie

Word
Roll 1 Number

1. Scream
2. Whimsical
3. Replicant
4. Corset
5. Faulty
6. Tingly

Character_____

Object _____Word _____

_____
_____
_____
_____
_____
_____
_____
_____
_____
_____
_____
_____
_____
_____
_____
_____
_____
_____
_____
_____
_____
_____
_____
_____
_____
_____
_____
_____
_____
_____
_____
_____
_____
_____
_____
_____

Character_____

Object _____Word _____

_____
_____
_____
_____
_____
_____
_____
_____
_____
_____
_____
_____
_____
_____
_____
_____
_____
_____
_____
_____
_____
_____
_____
_____
_____
_____
_____
_____
_____
_____
_____
_____

Character_____

Object _____Word _____

_____
_____
_____
_____
_____
_____
_____
_____
_____
_____
_____
_____
_____
_____
_____
_____
_____
_____
_____
_____
_____
_____
_____
_____
_____
_____
_____
_____
_____
_____
_____
_____
_____

Character_____

Object _____Word _____

Character_____

Object _____Word _____

_____
_____
_____
_____
_____
_____
_____
_____
_____
_____
_____
_____
_____
_____
_____
_____
_____
_____
_____
_____
_____
_____
_____
_____
_____
_____
_____
_____
_____
_____
_____

Character
Roll 1 Number

1. Lifeguard
2. ER nurse
3. Bounty hunter
4. Teen with a cloak
5. Daughter of an undertaker
6. Knitter

Word
Roll 1 Number

1. Aurora borealis
2. Taboo
3. Protection
4. Extinct
5. Mesmerizing
6. Descend

Scenario
Roll 1 Number

1. Cloudless sky turns black
2. MC wakes to find a pot of something boiling on stove
3. Holes are discovered in a backyard
4. Deep space vessel's computer wakes the crew too soon
5. Enchanted tree-house appears overnight
6. Swimming across a lake

Character_____Word_____
Scenario_____

_____
_____
_____
_____
_____
_____
_____
_____
_____
_____
_____
_____
_____
_____
_____
_____
_____
_____
_____
_____
_____
_____
_____
_____
_____
_____
_____
_____
_____
_____
_____
_____
_____

Character_____Word_____

Scenario_____

_____
_____
_____
_____
_____
_____
_____
_____
_____
_____
_____
_____
_____
_____
_____
_____
_____
_____
_____
_____
_____
_____
_____
_____
_____
_____
_____
_____
_____
_____
_____
_____
_____
_____
_____

Character_____Word_____
Scenario_____

_____
_____
_____
_____
_____
_____
_____
_____
_____
_____
_____
_____
_____
_____
_____
_____
_____
_____
_____
_____
_____
_____
_____
_____
_____
_____
_____
_____
_____
_____

Character_____Word_____
Scenario_____

_____
_____
_____
_____
_____
_____
_____
_____
_____
_____
_____
_____
_____
_____
_____
_____
_____
_____
_____
_____
_____
_____
_____
_____
_____
_____
_____
_____
_____
_____
_____
_____
_____
_____

Character_____Word_____
Scenario_____

_____
_____
_____
_____
_____
_____
_____
_____
_____
_____
_____
_____
_____
_____
_____
_____
_____
_____
_____
_____
_____
_____
_____
_____
_____
_____
_____
_____
_____
_____
_____
_____
_____
_____
_____
_____

CHARACTER DEVELOPMENT

Character
Roll 1 Number

1. Bookstore owner
2. Wedding planner
3. Elf with a hangover
4. Survivalist
5. Travel agent
6. Parole officer

Mood
Roll 1 Number

1. Gloomy
2. Dynamic
3. Erratic
4. Isolated
5. Frantic
6. Overwhelmed

Word
Roll 1 Number

1. Diabolical
2. Scatter
3. Wetware
4. Regret
5. Buoyant
6. Hang-up

Character_____

Mood_____Word _____

_____

_____

_____

_____

_____

_____

_____

_____

_____

_____

_____

_____

_____

_____

_____

_____

_____

_____

_____

_____

_____

_____

_____

_____

_____

_____

_____

_____

_____

_____

_____

Character_____

Mood_____Word _____

_____
_____
_____
_____
_____
_____
_____
_____
_____
_____
_____
_____
_____
_____
_____
_____
_____
_____
_____
_____
_____
_____
_____
_____
_____
_____
_____
_____
_____
_____
_____
_____
_____

Character_____

Mood_____Word _____

_____
_____
_____
_____
_____
_____
_____
_____
_____
_____
_____
_____
_____
_____
_____
_____
_____
_____
_____
_____
_____
_____
_____
_____
_____
_____
_____
_____
_____
_____
_____

Character_____
Mood_____Word _____
_____
_____
_____
_____
_____
_____
_____
_____
_____
_____
_____
_____
_____
_____
_____
_____
_____
_____
_____
_____
_____
_____
_____
_____
_____
_____
_____
_____
_____
_____
_____
_____
_____
_____
_____
_____

Character_____

Mood_____Word _____

_____

_____

_____

_____

_____

_____

_____

_____

_____

_____

_____

_____

_____

_____

_____

_____

_____

_____

_____

_____

_____

_____

_____

_____

_____

_____

_____

_____

_____

_____

_____

_____

_____

_____

Character
Roll 1 number
Even = MC is alone
Odd = Roll again for a companion

1. Wet nurse
2. Snowplow driver
3. Butcher
4. Taxidermist
5. Elf with a locket of human hair
6. Haunted house enthusiast

IF the MC is alone, add an object
Roll 1 Number

1. Charm bracelet
2. Wool blanket
3. Empty beer can
4. Fire extinguisher
5. Tape measure
6. Helmet

Scenario
Roll 1 number

1. Message in a fogged mirror
2. An unprotected gate
3. Trees along a trail begin to bleed
4. Running out of gas
5. Being interrogated by the police
6. Discovering an unscrewed light bulb

Character(s)_____

Object_____

Scenario_____

_____
_____
_____
_____
_____
_____
_____
_____
_____
_____
_____
_____
_____
_____
_____
_____
_____
_____
_____
_____
_____
_____
_____
_____
_____
_____
_____
_____
_____
_____
_____
_____

Character(s)_____

Object_____

Scenario_____

_____
_____
_____
_____
_____
_____
_____
_____
_____
_____
_____
_____
_____
_____
_____
_____
_____
_____
_____
_____
_____
_____
_____
_____
_____
_____
_____
_____

Character(s)_____

Object_____

Scenario_____

_____

_____

_____

_____

_____

_____

_____

_____

_____

_____

_____

_____

_____

_____

_____

_____

_____

_____

_____

_____

_____

_____

_____

_____

_____

_____

_____

_____

_____

Character(s)_____

Object_____

Scenario_____

_____

_____

_____

_____

_____

_____

_____

_____

_____

_____

_____

_____

_____

_____

_____

_____

_____

_____

_____

_____

_____

_____

_____

_____

_____

_____

_____

_____

_____

_____

Character(s)_____

Object_____

Scenario_____

_____

_____

_____

_____

_____

_____

_____

_____

_____

_____

_____

_____

_____

_____

_____

_____

_____

_____

_____

_____

_____

_____

_____

_____

_____

_____

_____

_____

_____

_____

_____

STORY DEVELOPMENT

Character
Roll 1 Number

1. Man with a scroll
2. Therapist
3. Jockey
4. Hotel pool attendant
5. Zombie
6. Ballerina

Trait
Roll 1 Number

1. Lucky
2. Calculating
3. Adventurous
4. Barren
5. Soft talker
6. Odd

Location
Roll 1 Number

1. Street minstrel show
2. Museum
3. Ski lodge
4. Breakdown lane
5. Jail cell
6. Hydroponics bay

Character_____Trait_____
Location_____

_____
_____
_____
_____
_____
_____
_____
_____
_____
_____
_____
_____
_____
_____
_____
_____
_____
_____
_____
_____
_____
_____
_____
_____
_____
_____
_____
_____
_____
_____
_____
_____

Character_____Trait_____
Location_____

_____
_____
_____
_____
_____
_____
_____
_____
_____
_____
_____
_____
_____
_____
_____
_____
_____
_____
_____
_____
_____
_____
_____
_____
_____
_____
_____
_____
_____
_____
_____
_____
_____

Character_____Trait_____
Location_____

_____
_____
_____
_____
_____
_____
_____
_____
_____
_____
_____
_____
_____
_____
_____
_____
_____
_____
_____
_____
_____
_____
_____
_____
_____
_____
_____
_____
_____
_____
_____
_____
_____

Character_____Trait_____
Location_____

Character_____Trait_____
Location_____

_____
_____
_____
_____
_____
_____
_____
_____
_____
_____
_____
_____
_____
_____
_____
_____
_____
_____
_____
_____
_____
_____
_____
_____
_____
_____
_____
_____
_____
_____
_____
_____
_____

STORY DEVELOPMENT

Character
Roll 1 Number

1. International student from Barcelona
2. Hiker
3. Shaman
4. Boy with flint
5. Traveling puppeteer
6. Police sketch artist

Object
Roll 1 Number

1. Reusable bag
2. Jack-o-lantern
3. Squeaky dog toy
4. Tea kettle
5. Corpse
6. Palm frond

Scenario
Roll 1 Number

1. Hairdresser is found with scissors in her neck
2. Tarot card reading
3. Given the wrong coffee order
4. Sudden decompression in a section of a space ship
5. Traveling to a fair
6. Fire ants invading a picnic

Character _____Object_____
Scenario _____

_____
_____
_____
_____
_____
_____
_____
_____
_____
_____
_____
_____
_____
_____
_____
_____
_____
_____
_____
_____
_____
_____
_____
_____
_____
_____
_____
_____
_____
_____
_____

Character _____ Object _____

Scenario _____

_____
_____
_____
_____
_____
_____
_____
_____
_____
_____
_____
_____
_____
_____
_____
_____
_____
_____
_____
_____
_____
_____
_____
_____
_____
_____
_____
_____
_____
_____
_____
_____
_____
_____
_____

Character _____Object_____

Scenario _____

_____
_____
_____
_____
_____
_____
_____
_____
_____
_____
_____
_____
_____
_____
_____
_____
_____
_____
_____
_____
_____
_____
_____
_____
_____
_____
_____
_____
_____
_____

Character _____Object_____

Scenario _____

_____
_____
_____
_____
_____
_____
_____
_____
_____
_____
_____
_____
_____
_____
_____
_____
_____
_____
_____
_____
_____
_____
_____
_____
_____
_____
_____
_____
_____
_____
_____
_____
_____

Character _____Object_____
Scenario _____

_____
_____
_____
_____
_____
_____
_____
_____
_____
_____
_____
_____
_____
_____
_____
_____
_____
_____
_____
_____
_____
_____
_____
_____
_____
_____
_____
_____
_____
_____
_____
_____

Character
Roll 1 Number

1. Fire spirit
2. Bookie
3. Paroled prisoner
4. Woman feeding ducks
5. Karate instructor
6. Serial killer

Object
Roll 1 Number

1. Camera
2. Flashlight
3. Piggy bank
4. Yellow #2 pencil
5. Raft
6. Sticky note

Word
Roll 1 Number

1. Background
2. Soothe
3. Impulse
4. Puncture
5. Decay
6. Wind

Character_____

Object _____Word _____

_____
_____
_____
_____
_____
_____
_____
_____
_____
_____
_____
_____
_____
_____
_____
_____
_____
_____
_____
_____
_____
_____
_____
_____
_____
_____
_____
_____
_____
_____
_____
_____

Character_____

Object _____Word _____

_____

_____

_____

_____

_____

_____

_____

_____

_____

_____

_____

_____

_____

_____

_____

_____

_____

_____

_____

_____

_____

_____

_____

_____

_____

_____

_____

_____

_____

Character_____

Object _____Word _____

_____
_____
_____
_____
_____
_____
_____
_____
_____
_____
_____
_____
_____
_____
_____
_____
_____
_____
_____
_____
_____
_____
_____
_____
_____
_____
_____
_____
_____
_____
_____
_____
_____

Character_____

Object _____Word _____

_____

_____

_____

_____

_____

_____

_____

_____

_____

_____

_____

_____

_____

_____

_____

_____

_____

_____

_____

_____

_____

_____

_____

_____

_____

_____

_____

_____

_____

_____

_____

_____

Character_____

Object _____Word _____

_____
_____
_____
_____
_____
_____
_____
_____
_____
_____
_____
_____
_____
_____
_____
_____
_____
_____
_____
_____
_____
_____
_____
_____
_____
_____
_____
_____
_____
_____
_____
_____

STORY DEVELOPMENT

Character
Roll 1 Number

1. Stablehand
2. Driving instructor
3. Long haul trucker
4. Computer coder
5. Hitchhiking hippie
6. Body builder

Word
Roll 1 Number

1. Injury
2. Emotion
3. Tethered
4. Special
5. Bump
6. Whiz

Scenario
Roll 1 Number

1. Setting up a campsite
2. Chasing a shadowy figure down an alley
3. Raven begins to speak
4. Hula hoop contest
5. Medical study takes an odd turn
6. In the audience of a talk show

Character_____Word_____
Scenario_____

_____
_____
_____
_____
_____
_____
_____
_____
_____
_____
_____
_____
_____
_____
_____
_____
_____
_____
_____
_____
_____
_____
_____
_____
_____
_____
_____
_____
_____
_____
_____
_____
_____

Character_____Word_____

Scenario_____

_____
_____
_____
_____
_____
_____
_____
_____
_____
_____
_____
_____
_____
_____
_____
_____
_____
_____
_____
_____
_____
_____
_____
_____
_____
_____
_____
_____
_____
_____
_____
_____

Character_____Word_____
Scenario_____

_____
_____
_____
_____
_____
_____
_____
_____
_____
_____
_____
_____
_____
_____
_____
_____
_____
_____
_____
_____
_____
_____
_____
_____
_____
_____
_____
_____
_____
_____
_____
_____

Character_____Word_____
Scenario_____

_____
_____
_____
_____
_____
_____
_____
_____
_____
_____
_____
_____
_____
_____
_____
_____
_____
_____
_____
_____
_____
_____
_____
_____
_____
_____
_____
_____
_____
_____
_____
_____
_____

Character_____Word_____
Scenario_____

_____
_____
_____
_____
_____
_____
_____
_____
_____
_____
_____
_____
_____
_____
_____
_____
_____
_____
_____
_____
_____
_____
_____
_____
_____
_____
_____
_____
_____
_____
_____
_____
_____

CHARACTER DEVELOPMENT

Character
Roll 1 Number

1. Guitar player
2. Rock climber
3. Courier
4. Vampire matchmaker
5. Boy with a dog
6. Assistant to a mad scientist

Mood
Roll 1 Number

1. Redemptive
2. Unimpressed
3. Complacent
4. Infatuated
5. Vacant
6. Antagonistic

Word
Roll 1 Number

1. Mingle
2. Toil
3. Humanity
4. Angelic
5. Fugitive
6. Remains

Character_____

Mood_____Word _____

Character_____

Mood_____Word _____

Character_____

Mood_____Word _____

_____

_____

_____

_____

_____

_____

_____

_____

_____

_____

_____

_____

_____

_____

_____

_____

_____

_____

_____

_____

_____

_____

_____

_____

_____

_____

_____

_____

_____

Character_____

Mood_____Word _____

Character_____

Mood_____Word _____

_____
_____
_____
_____
_____
_____
_____
_____
_____
_____
_____
_____
_____
_____
_____
_____
_____
_____
_____
_____
_____
_____
_____
_____
_____
_____
_____
_____
_____
_____
_____
_____
_____
_____

STORY DEVELOPMENT

Character
Roll 1 number
Even = MC is alone
Odd = Roll again for a companion

1. Stamp collector
2. Zombie trainer
3. Cake decorator
4. Lounge singer
5. Nurse in a psych ward
6. Electrician

IF the MC is alone, add an object
Roll 1 Number

1. Moped
2. Lens
3. 600-year-old amulet
4. Faraday cage
5. Fishing lure
6. Hard candy

Scenario
Roll 1 Number

1. Fortune teller goes missing
2. Archway appears with an unknown light source
3. Potluck after a wake
4. Car jacking
5. Yard far from water fills with shorebirds
6. Words begin to disappear from a spell book

Character(s)_____

Object_____

Scenario_____

_____
_____
_____
_____
_____
_____
_____
_____
_____
_____
_____
_____
_____
_____
_____
_____
_____
_____
_____
_____
_____
_____
_____
_____
_____
_____
_____
_____
_____
_____
_____

Character(s)_____

Object_____

Scenario_____

_____

_____

_____

_____

_____

_____

_____

_____

_____

_____

_____

_____

_____

_____

_____

_____

_____

_____

_____

_____

_____

_____

_____

_____

_____

_____

_____

_____

_____

_____

_____

_____

_____

_____

Character(s)_____

Object_____

Scenario_____

_____
_____
_____
_____
_____
_____
_____
_____
_____
_____
_____
_____
_____
_____
_____
_____
_____
_____
_____
_____
_____
_____
_____
_____
_____
_____
_____
_____
_____
_____
_____
_____
_____
_____
_____
_____

Character(s)_____

Object_____

Scenario_____

_____
_____
_____
_____
_____
_____
_____
_____
_____
_____
_____
_____
_____
_____
_____
_____
_____
_____
_____
_____
_____
_____
_____
_____
_____
_____
_____
_____
_____
_____
_____
_____
_____
_____
_____

Character(s)_____

Object_____

Scenario_____

_____
_____
_____
_____
_____
_____
_____
_____
_____
_____
_____
_____
_____
_____
_____
_____
_____
_____
_____
_____
_____
_____
_____
_____
_____
_____
_____
_____
_____
_____

READY TO TRY A DIFFERENT GENRE?

Check out the other books in the Roll-A-Prompt Writing Journal Series:

Mystery

Horror

Sci-Fi

Romance

Fantasy

For updates on new Roll-A-Prompt Writing Journals and periodic live writing prompt sessions, join our community at https://BookHip.com/FZHMZA

Made in the USA
Monee, IL
20 December 2020